BE CAREFUL
of
WHAT YOU
ASK

The Story of an Answered Prayer

Danny K. Corbitt, MD

Carpenter's Son Publishing

Be Careful of What You Ask

Published by Carpenter's Son Publishing, Franklin, Tennessee

Published in association with Larry Carpenter of Christian Book
Services, LLC
www.christianbookservices.com

Scripture taken from THE HOLY BIBLE, NEW INTERNATIONAL
VERSION®, NIV® Copyright © 1973, 1978, 1984, 2011 by Biblica,
Inc.™ Used by permission. All rights reserved worldwide.

Cover and Interior Design by Suzanne Lawing

Edited by Robert Irvin

Copy Edit by Adept Content Solutions

Printed in the United States of America

978-1-949572-30-8

CONTENTS

Introduction

AN ANSWERED PRAYER— JUST NOT AS I THOUGHT

Greetings! I'm thrilled you picked up this book. Please continue reading, not for the flowery prose or poetry you might hope to find because I am not a professional writer. Instead, read it for the confirmation that each of us has a need, a longing, a *desire* to more closely know the One who placed us here.

I don't know your circumstances or belief system, but I would love to share a story from firsthand knowledge. It is a story about how God answers prayers, a story about our human frailties, including our misconceptions and doubts. A story about how God showed me His unbounded love despite my attempts to achieve it on my own.

He's the reason you picked up this book.

You may agree that you need this confirmation of God's presence and promise to be with us. If that is the case, you will love the subtle and profound way He touched my life to drive home this fact.

This book, then, is for you.

On the other hand, you may feel you do not need this verification—that your life is just fine the way it is and that you do not need to be in a closer relationship with your Creator. It may be the least of your desires. Maybe you believe there is no God or that the God you knew previously has left you or allowed things to happen in your life that make it nearly impossible to trust again. If this is true, this book is especially for you.

Be patient as I try to explain, in my simple way, the circumstances of my eyewitness account of God's handiwork on my life. I think you will find the confirmation astounding.

I am a physician, an orthopedic surgeon. In December 2004, at the age of fifty, I had a bout with lung cancer—non-small cell adenocarcinoma stage IIB in my right lung. Although I am not a smoker, this is the form most commonly found in people who smoke. This news shook my world. There were events and happenings that surrounded this time that were inexplicable.

Coincidental?

Puzzling?

Timely?

No, the best description is: miraculous. I was a firsthand witness to God's mysterious marvels. I just did not recognize them at the time.

Looking back, it's clear to me He simply was answering a prayer request of mine in His own way and in His own time.

Be careful what you ask from God. He just might answer.

One

A Little Background Might Be Helpful

As I said in the Introduction, writing hasn't been my thing—not by a long shot. I am a retired orthopedic surgeon living in the Dallas–Fort Worth metroplex of North Texas. I practiced in the Lewisville/Flower Mound/Denton County area for thirty-one years.

I am married to Sallie, a strong, wonderful, godly woman I met in my last year of medical school. We have been married since April 1980. We have three outstanding children who have successfully escaped their parents' care. (When I was in my residency training, my attending physician always joked, "The true test of successful parenthood is when the child has survived long enough to be able to open the front door and get away!" I guess our children have surpassed that point in life.) All three have graduated from college and are flourishing in the adult world. We are blessed with three grandchildren, the joy of our lives.

I THOUGHT THIS WAS HOW THE WHOLE WORLD DID THINGS. MY CHILDHOOD WAS THE EPITOME OF NORMAN ROCKWELL'S SMALL-TOWN AMERICA!

I was born in Crockett, Texas, to a modest, loving couple who taught me and my two brothers the Bible as well as they could. My granddad and three uncles were ordained ministers, which meant all family gatherings eventually led to biblical stories and lessons. This was not necessarily a bad thing, but secular ideas outside of that sphere were met with only criticalness, sometimes followed by outright disdain and dismissal. I was taught to fear God and follow the Scriptures!

Still, leading a relatively sheltered childhood was great for me. I professed my belief in God and was baptized in the Southern Baptist tradition at age thirteen during a revival in a small East Texas church. I thought this was how the whole world did things. My childhood was the epitome of Norman Rockwell's small-town America!

All these things were my "normal," my comfort zone. It was the only life I knew. It certainly encompassed my whole world. Going to church and living the Golden Rule were as natural to me as breathing. "Do unto others as you would have them do unto you." I thought—

mistakenly—that everyone believed as I did. I was shielded from the majority of the world's behavior until I finished high school. I was a living example of Richie from the *Happy Days* television sitcom! I bet I can guess what you're thinking. Was I naive or what?

I graduated in 1972 as salutatorian of my high school class of 122 students, and I spent the next three years at Texas A&M University preparing for medical school. I was the first member of my extended family to receive a university degree, a feat that was subsequently matched by my brothers. Coming from a small school in East Texas where my entire graduating class was half the size of my first Chemistry 101 class at A&M, it was quite an accomplishment! My three years at A&M served as a springboard for application to medical school.

In short, I was living the American Dream.

I went from small-town USA to acceptance in med school at the University of Texas Medical Branch (UTMB)-Galveston in 1975. I'm betting that God had a hand in that as well, but that's a story for another day. As you may or may not know, medical school is not a place conducive to expanding your faith beliefs. Quite the contrary, we were encouraged to keep our faith and beliefs to ourselves. And, certainly as scientists and future physicians, most felt that a belief in God was the crutch of dependency used by the uneducated. The message was clear: there is little time to "waste" in pondering biblical questions or spending time with extended theological readings. Medical information flies fast and furious, and you just try to survive. With volumes of medical information to absorb, there is little time for the Bible. So, needless to say, my faith was placed on extended hiatus. I kept my beliefs to myself most of the time. It was easier that way.

NEEDLESS TO SAY, MY FAITH WAS PLACED ON EXTENDED HIATUS. I KEPT MY BELIEFS TO MYSELF MOST OF THE TIME. IT WAS EASIER THAT WAY.

Don't get me wrong; I loved medical school. Those were some of the best years of my life. I met lifelong friends and had a wonderful four years learning the intricacies of human anatomy, function, and pathology. This knowledge did have this effect: it solidified my belief in an ordered, fantastic creation from a higher order. It's amazing to me to see the human body, learn its functions, and observe its wonderful ability to heal itself and not believe in a higher power.

I'm a firm believer in this: the more we learn, the more there is to learn. Our bodies are intricate, delicate, and dependent—on both micro- and macro-environmental conditions to survive. Yet, our bodies are also durable and tough enough to withstand the forces of nature surrounding us. They are truly "fearfully and wonderfully made" (Psalm 139:14). I ask you to pardon my digression. I get excited when considering the marvels of this wonderful machine we call the human body!

* * * * *

I met, dated, and married Sallie, and eventually we moved to Fort Worth, where I completed my orthopedic residency in June 1985. My dream of a life was continuing. I joined a great group of orthopedic surgeons in the Lewisville/Flower Mound area and had a successful practice for the next several decades. I was attending church with my growing family, giving a decent amount of money to the church and charities, and I was there—some of the time, as you will see—to provide support for what I considered godly efforts. I was trying to live what I thought was the Christian life.

But to say my heart was where it needed to be would be a lie.

I was doing much of what I was doing for show.

I thought I was doing it for my family. Maybe it was for the image I thought I should present to my peers and the community. But I was merely going through the motions. It was a halfhearted attempt to construct a façade to fool others into thinking I was a good, moral person.

Throughout my childhood, I was taught that a father has to be the leader of his children and head of the family. I had been raised with the idea that we, as men, should be the providers for our family. The same idea included the expectation to work long hours to earn a better living than one's parents were able to provide. Does that sound familiar? It sounds like the mantra of a first-class baby boomer! I most definitely wanted to be the undisputed head of my family. Of course, that also required I be a follower of my wife's wishes! (I chuckle just a bit as I write that.) My dad raised me with this old adage: "If momma ain't happy, ain't nobody happy." So I tried to keep our family's momma happy! This meant we went to church to set the proper example for our children. It was the correct thing to do. Right?

And that brings us to the real reason for this story.

(As a final note in this opening chapter, it might be nice to have a Bible nearby as you read. I will have a number of references to Scripture throughout.)

Two

A Change in Priorities

Spring 2001. A colleague of mine had been insisting for about three years that I attend a three-day spiritual retreat called The Walk to Emmaus. I had tactfully avoided it by coming up with various excuses, usually at the last minute. But by the spring of that year, running out of reasons to decline, I reluctantly attended.

It was named Dallas Walk Number 147 and was held at Lake Lavon, Texas, in May of that year. It was a wonderful experience, filled with answers for which I had been searching for decades. Mainly, it reinforced my priorities. Being raised in East Texas by God-fearing parents, I believed my priorities were work, family, and God—in that order. After all, I had been charged by my father to work hard and care for my family. I had taken that very seriously, even too seriously. I had placed it at the top of my priority list—in front of family and God.

I would sacrifice time with my family for my occupational duties. For instance, every time we went out to eat as a family, we would take two cars because, inevitably, I would be called to the hospital to take care of someone or some problem that could not wait. It happened so often it became an ongoing joke with all of us. That would leave Sallie to bundle up the kids and put them to bed before I got home. I would arrive home in the wee hours of the morning to microwave the cold leftover dinner she had brought home from the restaurant hours earlier. And weekend rounds at the local hospitals would run late, causing me to be late to—or miss entirely—my children's games, plays, and other events.

MY DUTY TO MY PATIENTS ALWAYS CAME FIRST.

All the time, though, I was making good on my promise to my dad to work hard. At all costs, I was going to provide a good life for my wife and family! I allowed work to be a priority above other things.

My duty to my patients always came first.

My second priority was family. I tried to spend as much time as I could with them, even sacrificing Friday and Saturday golf games, so I could attend their weekend activities. And I thought all this was working. I was being a great dad with an acceptable compromise! And yet I was wrong. I was missing portions of the best years of their lives by making my work as an orthopedic surgeon my first priority. I didn't know any other way to handle it! Being on call meant being at the hospital—either in the ER, the operating room, or on some other floor—taking care of problems. During those years, our orthopedic group had a very busy practice, covering our entire county. There were times I took calls and covered four hospitals simultaneously, about thirty miles apart.

I especially remember one winter weekend. I did not go home for more than forty-eight hours. While working at one hospital, I would get called to another. I spent that entire weekend driving between hospitals taking care of emergencies; I never got home! Actually, at 4 a.m. one of those mornings, I did make it to my driveway—only to hear my beeper summoning me back to one of the hospitals for another emergency. I didn't even open the garage door. I backed out of the driveway and headed to the hospital.

My time with my family was suffering, but I was embodying the Puritan work ethic. Work hard, do not complain, and you will be rewarded. I just took the first part of that statement too literally.

Finally, there was God. He remained a distant third on my priority list. He would always be there if I needed Him, but He was never allowed to intrude on my daily affairs. Perhaps you are familiar with the concept: the white-bearded Ancient of Days somewhere in the heavens, holding court up there. He was the distant grandfather figure, benevolent in most things—and yet also displaying a nonyielding wrath of judgment for our transgressions. In my mind, He was an entity to be both loved and feared—but mostly feared. So I always kept Him at arm's length. I never allowed Him too close; I had areas in my life I wanted to keep for myself. You know, those little secrets we all have, those small corners of our hearts that love and hide our cherished and private feelings we refuse to give up. I did not feel a need to expose my problems, especially those He might have a problem forgiving! My life was going well. Why rock the boat? Besides, if I allowed Him to get too close, He might find out . . .

I believed in the "I'll call you if I need you" concept where God is an invisible genie who is able to give us all the wishes we ask. But I was not going to ask for trivial things. After all, as Creator and Master of the universe, He had other things, more important things, for which to care. And I was a wealthy, prosperous orthopedic surgeon with the means and ability to take care of most everyday things. I didn't think I needed any real contact with Him until something catastrophic happened.

> I BELIEVED IN THE "I'LL CALL YOU IF I NEED YOU" CONCEPT WHERE GOD IS AN INVISIBLE GENIE WHO IS ABLE TO GIVE US ALL THE WISHES WE ASK.

Do you see my dilemma? Perhaps yours, today, is similar. Maybe your priorities are like mine. Maybe you have other things that push God down the list of priorities in your life.

I had consciously pushed Him away to make room for what I thought were more important things: work and family. After all, I was that successful baby boomer determined to live the American dream!

* * * * *

On that weekend, on that Walk to Emmaus, I learned several things. But the one I remember most was the change in my priorities. When I returned home, my priorities had flipped. They had changed to a new order: God, family, and work now a distant third. Wow! Had my head spun around that quickly? Was I crazy? How was this new change going to affect my image in the community and with my colleagues and fellow workers at the office and the hospitals? For once in my life, I didn't care! I was convinced that my new order of priorities was correct, and I was going to invoke them no matter the cost. The Walk to Emmaus had given me a new perspective. I was a changed man. And I was determined to implement those changes immediately!

Remember the words of that famous "philosopher," Gomer Pyle? "Surprise, surprise, surprise!" It worked! My life became more ordered. The chaos that usually enveloped me on call and during my most difficult days at work was gone. I was still able to give my patients all the care they required. But it seemed there were more hours in the day to complete my tasks, and I still had time for my family!

I began to see God's handiwork in areas I had ignored before because I had been too busy. Do not ask me how that is possible; I just know it works! Keeping God first allowed all other things to fall into place. And all of it, somehow, did not seem to be dependent on any extra effort on my part. I was still living the same life with similar routines. It just happened.

I didn't understand it. I just happily followed.

Three

BE CAREFUL OF WHAT YOU ASK: THE PRAYER

After the Emmaus Walk was over, I received a gift from my mom's sister. My Aunt Violet sent me a leatherbound copy of Oswald Chambers's *My Utmost for His Highest*. It is a daily devotional book written seven decades ago by a young preacher. It begins on January 1 and has a daily lesson through December 31. My saintly aunt had written a note in the book, making it a keepsake that remains dear to my heart. In my newfound exuberance, fresh from The Walk to Emmaus, I began reading it as part of my daily routine. All was good.

Later that year, in December, I read a passage from *My Utmost* that shook the foundation of my beliefs. In fact, I read it three times. I could not believe what it said. How could a human write this? The profound information puzzled me. How could anyone follow these teachings? How did he know *my* situation some seventy years after this book was published? It was eerie. The devotional was called "The Test of Loyalty." The final paragraph caught my attention the most. So much that I circled it in red ink. It said:

HOW COULD ANYONE FOLLOW THESE TEACHINGS? HOW DID HE KNOW *MY* SITUATION SOME SEVENTY YEARS AFTER THIS BOOK WAS PUBLISHED?

The idea is not that we do work for God, but that we are so loyal to Him that He can do His work through us—"I reckon on you for extreme service, with no complaining on your part and no explanation on Mine." God wants to use us as He used His own Son.[1]

The passage hit me hard. What was Chambers saying? How could a human live so close to God that he would leave everything, not complain, and not expect some elaborate dissertation from the Almighty as to why he was asked to do this? I didn't understand. But what a concept! If it was possible, I wanted to be there. I desired to live with that depth of faith. I didn't really know what it would involve, but it didn't matter. That morning, regardless of the cost, regardless of the commitment, regardless of the requirements, I didn't care. Like the impetuous but lovable apostle Peter in the

Gospels, I was momentarily "all in."

I prayed a prayer that morning that I could live in a place so close to God that there would be no complaining from me and no explanation needed from Him. And exactly *where* was that? What would it mean? Could I have a relationship that close to the Almighty? One in which, no matter what He asked, I would not hesitate or make excuses? No matter the request, I would joyfully and obediently drop whatever I was doing and respond?

Was it—is it?—possible to exist in a relationship where I would not ask "why?" in response to His request? In proximity so intimate that He would not need to explain anything? I would simply accept the command and move forward to complete it. And what kind of existence is that? Is it achievable on this earth? It sounded like something only Jesus could do.

Nevertheless, I prayed that prayer.

That very morning,

I asked that very thing.

I prayed to live as one with Him, as He does with Jesus and the Holy Spirit (John 17).

I asked to accept His bidding without question and without explanation.

I prayed to be ready to step out in faith no matter the call.

I prayed without knowing the consequences or the costs.

I simply wanted to have that relationship with my God.

So, I have come to this conclusion: Be careful of what you ask. He just might give it to you!

Four

PERIOD OF SILENCE

Well, there you have it! I prayed the prayer to follow my Lord. He promised to give us anything we ask in His name (John 14:13). So it is done, end of story. Right?

Hardly.

For the next several years I continued in my walk without a perceptible difference in my daily surroundings or my apparent relationship with God. Don't get me wrong. Life was good. It just wasn't much different from the days before the prayer. I still was greatly involved in my church, trying to follow the commandment to love others, and I was spending more time with my family. But each year—yes, I continued to read my devotional book daily, starting over each January—I would return to the day in the book where

I first read the passage concerning "The Test of Loyalty" on December 18, 2001.

And each year I would ask myself if I had changed from the previous year. The answer, regrettably, was no. And it seemed there was a silence from God concerning this issue. It was almost laughable. Certainly, it was disconcerting. I had prayed to be placed at His right hand on a daily basis. Ready for any and all assignments and ready to change the world. I was a warrior anxious to unsheathe his sword to conquer evil and problems in this world. I was, like the apostle Peter, ready to walk on water.

EACH YEAR I WOULD ASK MYSELF IF I HAD CHANGED FROM THE PREVIOUS YEAR. THE ANSWER, REGRETTABLY, WAS NO. AND IT SEEMED THERE WAS A SILENCE FROM GOD CONCERNING THIS ISSUE.

Yet what I felt during these years was a growing, comfortable peace. There was a time of quietness. I existed in the mundane of the daily routine. The all-too-familiar place where we awaken, go to work, go home, eat dinner, and go to bed. Then repeat. Where is God in that?

I was in the valley, not on the mountaintop. But isn't that where most of our growth as believers takes place—in the valley? The mountaintop experiences are wonderful. But it is in the valley of day-to-day existence that we are shaped and prepared by God.

I didn't recognize it, but this was the calm before the storm.

I was studying regularly and going to various Bible classes. Hearing and absorbing sermons and lessons that were slowly but inevitably changing my life. I couldn't see it at the time, but the erosive process was

> I DIDN'T RECOGNIZE IT, BUT THIS WAS THE CALM BEFORE THE STORM.

in motion to wear down the obstacles in my life that were keeping me from the relationship with Him that I craved so much. Each year, on the day of my favorite devotional, I would be reminded in *My Utmost for His Highest* of my prayer request. But, with remorse, I would have to answer no to the question of whether my prayer had been answered. I could not see any change from the previous year in my relationship with God, nor in the life I was leading. It was a painstakingly slow process. I wasn't there yet, but I would continue. I was determined to achieve that level of intimacy with my Lord.

Notice how many times I said *I* and *my* in the last few sentences?

Time-out!

Could it be that *I* was the one responsible for the lack of response? Instead of trusting God to make the changes, was *I* the hurdle in this equation? In *my* determination to achieve a closer relationship, perhaps *I* was not allowing God to do His thing. *I* was not leaving Him room to prune the nonproductive branches in my life that were not living and therefore not part of

His plan (John 15:2). Could it be that *I* was the cause of the delay in hearing an answer to my prayer request? *I* wasn't helping. *I* was hindering. *I* was too busy trying to control my own satisfaction. But can an orthopedic surgeon, the captain of the operating room, give up that much control? *I* had spent my entire life trying to achieve exactly this position.

Control is a big thing to a surgeon. There were times in the operating room I would bring my fellow workers to tears if I felt they were not doing their jobs adequately. I demanded excellence and perfection for my patients and would accept nothing less. Laziness or ineptitude from my team was not acceptable. Rather, it would bring a tirade of expletives that would embarrass a sailor! And their dismissal from *my* operating room was not an infrequent event. I would not tolerate incompetence or excuses. That was great for my patients but not for my coworkers.

> CONTROL IS A BIG THING TO A SURGEON. THERE WERE TIMES IN THE OPERATING ROOM I WOULD BRING MY FELLOW WORKERS TO TEARS IF I FELT THEY WERE NOT DOING THEIR JOBS ADEQUATELY.

Now, I was willing to give up a sizable amount of control, but, at the same time, I always had to maintain some portion of that power. After all, it had been driven into my psyche since medical school.

"You are responsible."

"You are in control."

"It all comes back to you."

"You are the captain of the ship!"

I had been living in this pressurized crucible for more than twenty years. I can't give it up now—can I?

Would you?

Are you in the way of God's purpose in your life? By trying to do it all yourself, are you crowding Him out? I certainly was. In retrospect, I think I was the reason my prayer was not answered sooner. Had I been ready, I think He would have answered the prayer the moment it was spoken. However, as a hardheaded, resistant, controlling surgeon with an ego the size of my home state, I wasn't ready to enter that relationship.

And I didn't seem to be successful in achieving it on my own as evidenced by my Oswald Chambers devotional review each year. Each time, I would have to acknowledge my lack of progress. Remorsefully, I would have to answer no to noticeable changes in my relationship with God because *I* was in the way.

Five

THE KIDNEY STONE

It's time to fast-forward a few years. It was just before Christmas 2004. On a Friday night after dinner, Sallie and I were shopping for Christmas gifts for the kids' teachers. Walking down an aisle, I was hit with a sharp pain in my right flank. That is an anatomic term for the area of your back between the rib cage and the pelvis. The pain was instantaneous—then gone.

As a physician, I immediately tried to diagnose my pain with a list of potential reasons for it. Had I strained my back that day? Could it be appendicitis? Maybe it was the spicy Mexican food we had just finished at the restaurant! Alas, I told myself: no big deal.

Then it happened again and again *and again* in two- to three-minute intervals. I told Sallie I would wait for her in the car. The heated seats in the vehicle felt good but did not relieve the spasmodic, colicky, unrelenting, regularly recurring pain that was progressively getting stronger.

I spent the night at the foot of our bed, curled in a fetal position, pressing my back against the footboard of the bed in an attempt to relieve the pain. And as any good doctor would do, I continued to self-diagnose. It wasn't anterior (the front of my belly) in the right lower quadrant, which is typical of appendicitis. It wasn't in my hip or down my leg, either of which could be representative of sciatica or nerve-related pain. It could be kidney related, I told myself. Could it be a kidney stone? I had never experienced one before, but I knew the symptoms from my medical training. I had not had any recent episodes of strain to my lumbar area. It would be a stretch to attribute it to gastroenteritis, but that was a possibility.

With all these possibilities running through my mind, I was nauseous and miserable when, at sunrise, I woke up Sallie. I told her we needed to go to the emergency room. She agreed.

Upon arrival, I shuffled into the Medical Center of Lewisville ER and told my colleagues I was either having a baby or a kidney stone! My friend and fellow ER physicians laughed and directed us to the back of the department, where I was given an IV line for medications and the usual history, exam, and lab work to diagnose my illness. Remember, this is *my* ER! I had worked here for more than twenty years with many late nights and numerous orthopedic procedures, so I knew almost everyone on a first-name basis. I had even served on the board of trustees for the hospital for six years and was chief of surgery and chief of staff before that. Pretty impressive credentials, right?

The result that morning was that I was given VIP treatment!

After the exam and lab work were drawn, I had orders to get a KUB. That's an X-ray of the abdomen to look for problems with the kidneys, ureter, and bladder (hence KUB). This is most useful for finding kidney stones on a screening basis and was the standard of the day; it has now been commonly replaced by CT scanning in most facilities. After taking the KUB, the X-ray technologist asked me to step over to the chest X-ray machine for a routine chest X-ray. I was hurting and therefore not in a good mood. I proceeded to tell her I didn't need a CXR, that I was not there for my lungs, and that I was returning to the ER.

She questioned me. "But, Dr. Corbitt, a chest X-ray is ordered, and I will get in trouble if I don't do it." She pointed to the checked box on the radiology order form. Something snapped inside me! In an instant, I became a belligerent, uncompromising jerk. "How dare you question me, a physician? I could have you fired in a moment. I don't need a chest X-ray! And you are going to be in more trouble if you do it than if you don't!"

Not a very Christian response, was it?

I was feeling badly, very badly. That is still not a good excuse to act inappropriately to a courteous young woman who was simply doing her job. But I was tired. I was beyond arguing. And I was certainly in no mood to be questioned by a technician. As I was walking toward the door, the right flank pain instantly hit again—and buckled my knees.

I turned and told her, "Go ahead and take it. I will take it up with the ER doc when I get back. I don't feel like coming back later."

She complied, and I returned to the ER determined to confront my fellow physician concerning the CXR order.

When he came to my bedside to check on me, I asked why he had ordered the X-ray and actually accused him of trying to "pad the bill" since I had excellent insurance to cover my expenses. I'm sure you can understand my reaction. There are times doctors seem to add extra tests that are not entirely essential to a particular diagnosis. They order tests that might add some tangential information about the patient, but the results will not likely affect or change the diagnosis. They are following protocols to avoid missing some obscure condition that might be present but doesn't always obviously relate to the present illness.

HE LOOKED AT ME WITH A GLASSY-EYED STARE. HE WAS BEWILDERED AND CONFUSED. YOU KNOW THE LOOK I'M DESCRIBING.

Was I a jerk or what? I was accusing a colleague of an act he would never willingly commit! He had no reason to order a test that was not needed. He was a very intelligent guy, and I was not the first person he had seen with an apparent kidney stone. He was only doing his job. I was not exactly a shining example of the forgiving Christian.

He looked at me with a glassy-eyed stare. He was bewildered and confused. You know the look I'm describing. It's the look in which someone peers right through you without acknowledging your presence. As if you are not really there at all. Then he said, "Chest X-ray? I didn't order a chest X-ray. Why would I order a chest X-ray? I ordered a KUB."

And he walked away, muttering to himself.

I came to the only conclusion that seemed appropriate at that time: "Idiot."

After all, I had seen the chest X-ray box marked on the request. How could he say he didn't order it? Was it a simple mistake? Had he checked the wrong box? Or had *Someone* checked it for him? Maybe it was a "God wink."[2] Maybe you have had one of those special moments when, inexplicably, something happens that makes you wonder if something or someone is watching over you. You may have avoided an accident by the thinnest of margins. Maybe something told you to not enter what became a dangerous situation. Some like to think they have a guardian angel watching over them.

For me, this was one of those moments. But at the time, it slipped right by me.

As a physician, I knew the essential aspects of the workup of a kidney stone. Since I was having no chest or lung symptoms and did not have an acute abdominal picture, the abdominal KUB X-ray was essential, but the CXR was not. The only help a chest X-ray would have added was determining the presence of air under the diaphragm from a perforated ulcer, but then I would be exhibiting a whole different set of symptoms and a completely different physical exam. One with a rigid abdomen and extreme abdominal pain, a picture of peritoneal involvement, not the spasmodic right flank pain I was experiencing. In a fifty-year-old male non-smoker, a CXR was useful baseline information for lung issues but hardly essential in the diagnosis of a kidney stone.

At that point, I was exhausted. So I accepted my treatment, returned home, and, not surprisingly, passed a kidney stone later that afternoon.

I had a follow-up appointment with my urologist the next week, so I thought the crisis was over.

Six

The Moment of Truth

Having passed the kidney stone, I was feeling much better and returned to work as usual on Monday morning. About midmorning, I received a phone call from the hospital's radiology department. Our offices were on the second floor of the hospital medical office building, which made our interaction very efficient. The radiologist, a good friend, began to ask several questions that brought alarm.

"Dan, are you having any shortness of breath or cough?" she asked.

"No."

She continued. "Have you coughed up any blood?"

Troubled, I answered, "No."

Her last question: "Have you lost any weight?"

I was confused. "Liz, these are not very good questions."

She sighed. "I'm not looking at a very good X-ray," she said. "You need to come down here now."

I found a stopping place in my clinic schedule and sprinted downstairs to the X-ray department. As I entered the door to her office, I was stopped in my tracks by the chest X-ray hanging on her view box. Have you ever seen a rattlesnake, after previously encountering one, and immediately recognized it? Was there a doubt in your mind as to what it was? No, if something like that happens, it is immediate and chilling! It freezes you physically!

That's exactly how I felt that morning. The chest X-ray hanging on the view box showed a tumor in the right upper lobe of the lung, about 3 to 4 centimeters in diameter. What I was looking at was unmistakable.

Poor soul, I thought.

Then it hit me. "Liz. That's not mine?"

Her reply shook my world. "Yes, I'm afraid so." My heart fell into my pelvis. *No, this cannot be.* I don't smoke. I have intentionally never so much as tasted a cigarette. The association of smoke and lung cancer had been driven into all of us in medical school. I never wanted anything to do with those nasty things. So how could I now have lung cancer? How could this be *my* X-ray? Yet here I was, looking at a mass in my right lung that could not carry a good prognosis. I couldn't be sure it was a malignancy by the X-ray alone, but it did not have the appearance of a benign nodule or infiltrate. It was not pneumonia. There was no effusion. Cancer has an appearance all its own!

Suddenly, all my medical school knowledge began

swirling in my consciousness. I began to recall all the statistics of survival rates for lung cancer and the treatment modalities that would be required over the next few months. I remembered previous patients who had succumbed to this dreaded disease. I knew the details of the course of this disease personally; my wife and I both lost our fathers to lung cancer, in 1985 and 1987, respectively. We watched them lose their battles in the first four months after their diagnoses. Yes, you could say I was officially in a state of panic!

Liz continued. "You need a pulmonologist and a chest surgeon," she told me. I could hardly swallow, but I replied, "I think you are right."

I didn't tell anyone for a few days. No need to disrupt my schedule and create unnecessary worry for my staff and patients, but I could not keep it from Sallie. Her perception skills are far too keen. She knew something was wrong. When I told her, she became the rock I would come to lean on for the rest of my treatment. I knew she was tough. Her German ancestry endowed her with a very stoic nature. Through three childbirths, broken bones, plenty of scrapes, and multiple illnesses, she had always shown her resilience. But this was different. It had *finality* to it. Her reply to me that day was concise, emphatic, and calculated.

She maintained her com-

SHE MAINTAINED HER COMPOSURE FOR THE BOTH OF US, THEN SAID, "WELL, LET'S GET ON WITH IT. IT WILL BE ANOTHER NEW ADVENTURE!"

posure for the both of us, then said, "Well, let's get on with it. It will be another new adventure!"

Did she know something I didn't? Over the next few months, Sallie never wavered. I assume she was as devastated as I was, but she refused to show it. Was her faith shaken? Surely it was, but she never hesitated. She never broke down in any way that I could see. Her determination to see this thing through was rock solid. We *were* in for a new adventure. Our course was set; we just had to hang on! And what a course it was. Things began to happen fast and furiously.

I would like to write something regarding the spouses or significant others who are close to someone who receives this type of diagnosis. They are forced to go through this nightmare through no choice on their part, in the same manner as the patient. For this reason, I think the spouses may be subject to *more* fear and stress than the involved patient simply from the standpoint of having to face the possible loss of a loved one and being forced to continue alone. I'm not lessening in any way the plight of the person diagnosed with a terminal disease. From a personal standpoint, it is sheer terror! But I have become very sympathetic to the situation of the spouse, partner, and family members who are confronted with the likelihood of being alone in the near future. And having to deal with the mundane tasks that, not so long ago, were the duties of their deceased loved one. God bless you all!

* * * * *

It was the Christmas season of 2004. We made it through Christmas for our kids, who were young adults and teenagers at the time. Our son was in college and my two daughters still in high school. How do you protect your children from such awful news? Sallie and I tried to downplay our distress as much as possible. We didn't think it wise to offer details of the pending diagnosis until all information was available to avoid disrupting our kids' lives and routines. Some parents might argue this point, as is your right, but we felt it best to allow them to function as normally as possible until circumstances made it necessary to adapt to any changes that might occur.

HOW DO YOU PROTECT YOUR CHILDREN FROM SUCH AWFUL NEWS? SALLIE AND I TRIED TO DOWNPLAY OUR DISTRESS AS MUCH AS POSSIBLE.

We had a family meeting one evening just before my surgery was scheduled to outline the reason I was having a procedure. I told them I had a growth on my lung and was scheduled to have a biopsy to remove it and determine its identity. I didn't offer any details on the prognosis or complications since they were still basically unknown. We offered hope that everything would work out for the best and tried to keep them from worrying. As always, we left the conversation open for questions. There were none.

For our family, this choice was the right one and had the effect we desired. In retrospect, a conversation with my son and older daughter years later revealed that neither was overly worried about my condition at the time. Only later, when my middle daughter was in pharmacy school, was she made aware of the statistics of my condition. Sometimes, as physicians, we know too much. Maybe Sallie and I tried to insulate our children too much at the time of the event, but that was our decision, and I'm glad we chose it. After all, there was nothing they could do to change the problem. And their worrying would only add to the stress Sallie and I were already facing. Despite our inadequacies in parenting, all three of our children have turned out to be wonderful young adults.

My workup was delayed a few weeks because of the holidays; the waiting time was horrible. But this delay helped me become more aware of my patients' points of view from years past, when my schedule would cause them to have to wait for treatment. Their fear and anxiety would multiply. My wait was disturbing. But I could better appreciate their perspective now that I was a patient in need of news and treatments.

My first assistant, Beth, also was not fooled by my demeanor. Because I needed to make time in my schedule for appointments for testing and to see other doctors, she

> SHE ASKED ME SEVERAL TIMES WHAT WAS GOING ON, AND I TRIED TO DEFLECT THOSE QUESTIONS WITH LITTLE WHITE LIES. IT DIDN'T WORK. I GUESS SHE SAW IT ON MY FACE.

quickly picked up on my problem. She asked me several times what was going on, and I tried to deflect those questions with little white lies. It didn't work. I guess she saw it on my face. This happens with someone who has been with you for more than ten years when you are not a good liar. She did a commendable job of maintaining her emotions and promised to keep me in her prayers. Then she promptly began to take over management of my practice and patients, a job she continued during the next several months. My entire office was extremely supportive for the duration of the illness. I was blessed to be surrounded by such wonderful people.

* * * * *

Sallie and I met with the pulmonologist, and he quickly agreed this looked like cancer. He ordered a CT scan to confirm the size and location of the tumor. We also did a PET scan to rule out metastases, or spread of the tumor. The PET scan showed the primary tumor in the right lung, consistent with a malignancy, and some small areas that were not conclusive of either early degenerative processes or small areas of possible tumor. But these tests were not enough to show the type of tumor, so a biopsy would have to be done. Our decision was to proceed with the consult to a cardiothoracic surgeon.

I made two phone calls. The first was to my trusted friend, our family practitioner, to ask his opinion on a cardiothoracic surgeon. Without hesitation, he said, "Larry Schorn, in Irving."

Next, I called on my respected internal medicine

physician/friend of twenty years and told him the story of a fifty-year-old male with a mass in the right lung. He read through the lines quickly. "Dan, is this you?" he asked. After I confessed, he prayed with me and told me there was only one cardiothoracic surgeon he would recommend: "Larry Schorn."

I made the call.

Dr. Larry Schorn is a very busy man. He had, at that time, an extremely vibrant practice in Irving, Texas. Rather than wait for a scheduled appointment, which might have taken months, he told me to meet him the next day at the Grapevine hospital where he would be operating. Sallie and I grabbed the scans and records and drove to Grapevine. About 6 p.m., after a full day of surgery, Dr. Schorn met us in the waiting room, and we went back with him to review the studies. His response was quick, deliberate—and crushing. He said it did appear to represent a tumor, not an infection or fungal mass. He continued: "It needs to come out."

HIS RESPONSE WAS QUICK, DELIBERATE— AND CRUSHING. HE SAID IT DID APPEAR TO REPRESENT A TUMOR, NOT AN INFECTION OR FUNGAL MASS.

He was scheduled to go on a medical mission trip to Central America the next week but said he would insert me in his operating room schedule the week he returned. He planned to do a thorascopic exam first for biopsy and/or an excision with an open thoracotomy if the scope was inadequate. Here's what that means in layman's terms: this is a laparoscopic procedure to assess the tumor and possibly biopsy it if it is accessible. He would follow that with an open surgery into the chest to remove it along with the surrounding lung tissue, depending on the pathologic diagnosis.

Despite the stunning news, I was comforted knowing his expertise and faith in God as evidenced by his mission obligations. The reassurance of having a man dedicated to his faith is incredible. So it was quite acceptable to wait for his return from the medical mission to address my needs. There was a sense of peace and confirmation that we had found the right guy. As a matter of fact, the perceived delay of a week until his return was a blessing, not a curse. I needed that time for some things to occur that, without my knowledge, would present themselves before my surgery.

Did God have a hand in this? You know, being in the right place at the right time? Crossing paths with someone you've never met just when you might need their services? We have all had those moments, such as thinking of someone we have not had contact with in a long time, only to answer a call and find them on the other end of the line! Or being delayed getting to an event and finding out later there was an accident or tragedy that would have involved us if we had left at our scheduled time. That inexplicable moment where, beyond our control, something happens that benefits us without our knowledge.

And what is the most miraculous thing of all, as I

see it? Both my friends and colleagues recommended the same surgeon. They did so without hesitation or any reservation. When, I might ask, have you ever heard of two doctors independently agreeing on the same thing instantaneously and without hesitancy? Ask any physician—that is a miracle in itself!

These things are easier to see in retrospect, but everything was happening too fast for me to stop and ponder it all in the winter of 2004–2005. At the time, none of this appeared like a God Moment to me!

Seven

THE LESSON OF ABRAHAM

Over the next ten days, I tried to maintain a normal life, but that's pretty much impossible in these circumstances. The worry of the pending surgery, and, more importantly, the prognosis of lung cancer were hanging over my head like the proverbial sword of Damocles from ancient Greek literature.

On Tuesday mornings I usually attended a Bible study led by Rev. Tommy Nelson at one of our local churches. Rev. Nelson is an excellent teacher, and we were studying the Proverbs. But on the next Tuesday morning, Tommy was ill, and a young student would step in for the lesson. As Bernard, the protégé, took the lectern, he apologized. He said we would not be continuing in Proverbs that morning. He felt led, he said, to give another lesson for someone in the group who was in need. He continued, saying, "I don't know what the problem is exactly. It might be job-related, a marital problem—*heck, it might even be cancer!*" What! How did he know? I had not told anyone, not even my closest friends who sat only a few feet away. Who was this guy? And what did he know about my recent diagnosis? I was about to be blown away!

He asked us to turn to Genesis chapter 22. After that everything began to blur. I might as well have been the only one in the room. It seemed he was looking at and speaking directly to me. This lesson was meant for me. The story, as you may know, is the time when God tested Abraham. I wrote furiously; I was trying to keep up. I was bewildered at the circumstances of the correlation of this lesson to my plight. I will try to recreate the details of this lesson as closely as possible. To begin, I apologize for the fragmentary nature, but these are from my original notes of that early morning lesson. It would probably be helpful if you open a Bible to Genesis chapter 22 and follow. All of my biblical references are from the NIV version, unless noted otherwise.

In Genesis 22:1, God tests Abraham. He doesn't tempt him, since temptation comes from Satan, not God. James 1:13 tells us that God cannot be tempted with evil, and neither does He tempt any man. Satan tempts, the world tempts, and we tempt ourselves. This is verified in 1 Corinthians 7:5. But God does not tempt. Hearing the call from God in verse 1 of Genesis 22, Abraham answers with a servant's heart: "Here I am." It is interesting to note that three of the other patriarchs of the Old Testament—Moses, Samuel, and Isaiah—also answered God's call in the same fashion: "Here I am."

Little did I realize at this time that I was undergoing a similar test of my faith with the recently diagnosed cancer in my right lung. How would *I* answer?

Genesis 22:2: "Take your son, your only son, Isaac, whom you love, and go to the region of Moriah. Sacrifice him there as a burnt offering on one of the mountains I will tell you about."

LITTLE DID I REALIZE AT THIS TIME THAT I WAS UNDERGOING A SIMILAR TEST OF MY FAITH WITH THE RECENTLY DIAGNOSED CANCER IN MY RIGHT LUNG. HOW WOULD *I* ANSWER?

This doesn't make sense. It's *not logical.*

The reason it is not logical comes with the knowledge that God had just made a covenant with Abraham concerning the abundance of Isaac's progeny. Isaac had to survive to fulfill that covenant, which is found in Genesis 17:7. Throughout history, God has never broken a covenant. The "only son" is a prophetic reference to Jesus Christ, the *only* begotten Son of God. Please refer to one of my favorite verses in the entire Bible, John 3:16 (KJV): "For God so loved the world that He gave His only begotten Son, that whosoever believeth in Him should not perish, but have everlasting life."

Second, God had never before demanded human sacrifice. He condemned it as pagan worship in Deuteronomy 12:31! Yet here he *commands* Abraham to take his son Isaac and sacrifice him on Mount Moriah, which is very interesting, and prophetic.

Mount Moriah is the site of the Temple Mount in Jerusalem described in 2 Chronicles 3:1. Why would God pick that particular place to have Abraham sacrifice Isaac? Because it was a clue to a future event! What else was sacrificed on "one of the mountains" in the region of Moriah, some two thousand years later? This represents a foreshadowing of the crucifixion of Christ in the distant future at the exact same location! Is our God a stickler for details? I think so![3]

From here, I will leave Bernard's devotional that morning and pick up the story the best I can in my words.

This tendency of God to take care of small details would become evident later in my story when He would confirm with me the knowledge He had of my needs and concerns. But on this morning, all of that was lost in the rapid, spinning confusion I was experiencing with the upcoming surgery for the cancer in my chest.

In Genesis 22:3 we read, "Early the next morning . . ." Note there is no hesitation or procrastination on Abraham's part. No excuses. He doesn't ask: "Why?" He just saddles the donkeys and goes. He could have taken two or three weeks, a month, or even several years to follow the command. But he doesn't. He leaves "early the next morning." Now, remembering what I prayed for in December 2001, didn't I ask to live in that same obedience as Abraham? I prayed to be willing to follow God's direction "with no questions on my part, and no explanation needed on His." That is exactly what

Abraham did, and without delay.

But still I did not get it. Unlike Abraham, I was not ready to drop everything and follow a command from God. Not without, at the very least, some questioning on my part. And certainly not without requiring an explanation of the details or plan of action. For heaven's sake, I am an orthopedic surgeon! I never enter a situation without a detailed plan. And usually with two or three backup plans in case Plan A fails! Surely such blind obedience could not apply to me!

> FOR HEAVEN'S SAKE, I AM AN ORTHOPEDIC SURGEON! I NEVER ENTER A SITUATION WITHOUT A DETAILED PLAN. AND USUALLY WITH TWO OR THREE BACKUP PLANS IN CASE PLAN A FAILS!

In Genesis 22:5 the story continues. Abraham says, quite simply, "*We* will worship, and then *we* will come back to you."

The italics are mine, to emphasize the depth of what Abraham said. This is the ultimate in faith as evidenced in Hebrews 11:17, where it reads, "By faith Abraham, when he was tried, offered up Isaac; and he that had received the promises offered up his only begotten son, of whom it was said, 'That in Isaac shall thy seed be called'" (KJV). Abraham either felt Isaac would be spared or restored—resurrected!—and they *both* would return. He had the faith to tell his servants before going up the hill, "We will come back to you."

One of my favorite verses is Genesis 22:7. "But where is the lamb?" Young Isaac asks the question, and he sums up the entire Old Testament with this one inquiry. All the patriarchs, judges, kings, and prophets asked the same question: "Where is the lamb?" It is answered in John 1:29 (KJV) when John the Baptist proclaims, "Behold the Lamb of God, which taketh away the sin of the world." He is referring to none other than Jesus, the Christ. So again, here is another referral, in prophecy, to Jesus, who would come to earth about two millennia later.

So we come to Genesis 22:9, and we may wonder why Isaac didn't resist. He was obviously a *lot* younger than Abraham—faster and stronger. Yet he allowed himself to be bound on the altar. Does this remind us of Jesus giving His life willingly, as He talked about in John 10:18 (KJV): "No man taketh it from me, but I lay it down of myself. I have power to lay it down, and I have power to take it up again. This commandment have I received of my Father." Jesus willingly gave His life for us!

Then in Genesis 22:13 we read, "Abraham looked up." What he saw was the sacrifice, a ram, caught in the thicket. Please note the sacrifice provided was not a lamb, but a *ram*. This is important because this was the sacrificial animal needed to ordinate a priest as noted in Leviticus 8:22. Could this possibly be a reference to our High Priest, Jesus Christ, who is described as such in Hebrews 4:14–16? Continuing, we read, "Instead of . . ." This is the first mention of a substitutionary sacrifice, which is seen numerous times in the Old and New Testaments until the death of Christ on the cross. Jesus willingly substituted Himself for us for the atonement of our sins.

Can you imagine my confusion after this lesson? Needless to say, I saved all the notes from that day and have shared some of them with you. It's a wonderful lesson that was directed, I believe, *straight at me*! I have no doubt that God provided it. But at that time I could not see the application that the lesson provided. Remember the prayer I prayed some three years earlier? I had asked to be so close to God that I would agree to anything he asked. I would ask no questions; I would demand no explanation.

Isn't this exactly what Abraham did? He answered with just three words: "Here I am," with no questions, procrastination, or hesitation. He didn't wait for an explanation to the completely illogical request from God to kill his only son! Isaac was the son who had been promised to be the continuation of the line of the nations (Genesis 17:7). Abraham had waited one hundred years for a son to continue his lineage only to be told that son would be sacrificed on an altar! And he was ready to comply without argument or the need for explanation.

THE PRECISE ATTENTION TO DETAIL SHOWS THAT GOD KNOWS US AND HAS A PLACE IN OUR LIVES ON A DAILY BASIS— IF WE ONLY ALLOW HIM TO TAKE IT.

Wow! What faith!

The precise attention to detail shows that God knows us and has a place in our lives on a daily basis—if we only allow Him to take it.

I didn't make the correlation that morning to my prayer request of December 2001 following the reading of my devotional book. But the lesson was undeniable. If I wanted to live in the closeness exhibited by Abraham, which was exactly the essence of my prayer, I would have to be willing to sacrifice everything dear to me so that nothing stood between me and God.

But events were too complicated, and my mind was not in the right place to make the correlation at that time. In retrospect, what a wonderful lesson God provided that morning for my problems. No doubt a reminder sent to confirm that He had heard my prayer from three years before. He was faithfully answering my prayer, and I didn't even know it! The only problem was that I was not ready. I had too many issues that were standing between us.

And the major one was still . . . me.

Eight

MY EPIPHANY

After the lesson on Abraham, I found myself blindly stumbling through the next week awaiting the surgery scheduled with Dr. Schorn. I was confused concerning the reason God would allow this to happen to me. And the timing! Given the fact I had a son in college and two daughters still at home, it was terrifying. I was only fifty years old. I was in the prime of life for a surgeon.

What if the tumor was malignant? All the tests we had completed certainly seemed to point in that direction. What if I followed the statistics for most lung cancers of this type and didn't survive the first two years? What would happen to my wife and children? What about my patients? My practice? All these questions, and many more, were swirling in my head day and night.

I had no rest.

I was exhausted.

And I was scared. No, it was beyond that. I was terrified!

Early one morning, before sunrise, I crept into my closet. In the quiet darkness, I fell to my knees and assumed a fetal position. Curled in a ball, I began praying to the only One I had left. I didn't have words at first. I was angry at God. Confusion, betrayal, and sheer terror gripped me as I argued before God. I had no symptoms, no pain, and no signs of the malignancy that was enlarging in my chest. Why would He allow me to have a tumor that could possibly take my life? Had I not professed my belief at age thirteen? Had I not tried to live a good life during my high school and college years? Even in medical school, when I was so quiet and remote with my faith, I never denied His presence. Now, in recent years, I had been attending church with my family. I was tithing to the church and giving to charity. Heck, I had even attended the Walk to Emmaus! What else could He ask of me? These things should count for something! What more could He want?

"God, none of this makes sense!" I finally shouted that morning, defiantly.

That was certainly not the response of Abraham to God's command in Genesis 22, was it? But like the test He gave Abraham, this made no sense. It wasn't logical. It was a shock. I wasn't prepared for something like this!

By this time, I was yelling at Him. I was confused and desperate, still trying to make my case for justice, not realizing that I needed *mercy* instead. I was terrified with the knowledge of my prognosis. It was a harsh one if the tumor was malignant. I knew, as a physician, that the survival rate for stage II cancer (greater than 3 centimeters) was around 45 percent for five years and less than 14 percent if there was any spread beyond the primary site. I knew that by the time a tumor this size was seen on an X-ray, 55 percent of the time it had already started spreading to other areas of the body. A tumor the size of mine, in stage II, raised the likelihood that metastasis was present. Any spread of the tumor beyond its primary margins would exponentially raise the mortality rate.

I was aware that these statistics were about to be determined for me with the outcome of the biopsy/excisional surgery pending in a few days. The scary thing was that

I WAS AWARE THAT THESE STATISTICS WERE ABOUT TO BE DETERMINED FOR ME WITH THE OUTCOME OF THE BIOPSY/EXCISIONAL SURGERY PENDING IN A FEW DAYS. THE SCARY THING WAS THAT I WAS NO LONGER IN CONTROL.

I was no longer in control.

I was an orthopedic surgeon for heaven's sake! I had money to get treatment anywhere in the world. I had peers, colleagues, and partners in the medical world to get the best outcome. I had the means to the best doctors the world had to offer. I could afford to travel anywhere on the planet to get help. I had the ability to control my destiny. Except . . .

Except I was presented with a diagnosis, a problem, where none of that mattered. I was in the United States, which has the best medical knowledge on the planet. I was living in a place with the best doctors, testing, and treatment available to anyone. But the results would be no different. The statistics would not change. The outcome was out of my control. And it scared me like nothing ever had in my lifetime.

I tried "Let's Make a Deal" with God that morning. I offered Him all I could think of to change this process. If He would take it away, I would serve Him more than I had in the past. I would give more to the church. I would help with the youth. I would go on mission trips to third-world countries to help the poor. I had wealth, power, influence, relationships, and prestige. I would do all of that for Him if He would just take

EXHAUSTED, SWEATING, AND TREMBLING WITH FEAR, I FINALLY GAVE UP. I TOLD HIM, "LORD, I'M DONE. I HAVEN'T GOT ANYTHING ELSE TO GIVE." I SURRENDERED.

this tumor away.

But in the darkness there was only silence.

Exhausted, sweating, and trembling with fear, I finally gave up. I told Him, "Lord, I'm done. I haven't got anything else to give." I surrendered.

BAM! It was as if I had said the magic password! In the silence, I felt a presence.

At that moment, He hugged me! I promise I am not crazy (although my friends may think so). I felt the presence of someone wrapping me in a blanket of warmth. Remember on a cold winter night, the feeling of comfort and safety when your parents would wrap you in their arms? It is a feeling like no other.

It was just like that. He enveloped me in a gentle embrace.

A bear hug. No, a *God hug!*

The warmest, most comfortable, snuggly feeling you could imagine.

There were no angelic choruses, no rainbow lights, no rumblings of thunder. Just the sweetest, most intimate moment you can experience. One that consoles and comforts you with a peace that cannot be explained!

Then a pair of hands took my face. Cradling it ever so gently, I could feel someone peering into my face as a parent would to a crying child. I saw nothing but brightness through my closed eyelids. I didn't see any facial features. But I heard the most beautiful voice of my lifetime, a quiet, reassuring whisper:

"It will be all right. It will be all right."

Then it was gone. In an instant.

But the impact of that voice was timeless.

I wanted to shout. The heavy burden was lifted! My heart was light as a feather. What a liberating, freeing feeling! No worries. Nothing else mattered. The things that just moments ago were causing such agony were suddenly unimportant.

The voice did not promise I would not die. It didn't promise I would not trudge through the ordeal that was looming on the horizon with surgery and the chemo-therapy that would follow. It only stated, "It will be all right." No matter the outcome, He had told me not to worry anymore. He had this. He was in control instead of me. It was no longer just my problem. Now He would share the journey with me. He didn't promise to take the problem away; He promised to take me through it.

If I died, I would be with Him. Like the thief on the cross to Jesus' right, I would immediately be with Him in Paradise (Luke 23:43).

"It will be all right."

If I lived, no matter the consequences, He would be there to walk with me.

"It will be all right."

In that moment, I essentially surrendered all rights to myself. As a physician, I knew the likely outcome of the cancer in my chest. Although we had not found any spread of the tumor to that point, I knew the statistics. I knew the natural history of most lung cancers. Why would I be any different? I think it was easier for me to face the terror once I had confirmation of His presence.

So for all the days to follow, nothing else matters. All things pale in comparison to this promise. It's as real today as that morning I first heard it. Even today, as I write these words, it is still "all right"! He still walks this journey with me as He promised that morning.

Surely that is what the apostle Paul meant when he wrote his letter to the Philippians (4:7): "And the peace of God, which surpasses all understanding, will guard your hearts and minds through Christ Jesus." I had been given the peace that is beyond description. So no matter what I would face in the coming days, He would be there to "guard my heart and mind."

Jesus never promised us there would be no hardships or troubles. On the contrary, He said just the opposite. "In the world you will have tribulation. But take heart, I have overcome the world" (John 16:33, KJV). And He left us with the promise in Matthew 28:20 (KJV), where He says, "And lo, I am with you always, even unto the end of the world."

So no matter what comes, He is with us. We should never lose hope regardless of the situation. Just because things go terribly wrong and our outlook may be bleak, He is still there and has been all along.

He is waiting.

Waiting for our call for help.

Waiting for us to surrender the right to ourselves.

Waiting for us to come home.

Then nothing else matters because: *"It will be all right."*

Nine

THE SURGERY

The day of surgery had arrived. It was January 19, 2005. I don't remember any important details before the procedure except one: I was surprisingly calm inside. With my recent epiphany, it seemed the surgery would be a routine event regardless of the news we would learn. I remember the pre-op room. My pastor was there, along with my sister-in-law, Mollie. Sallie and I had prayer with them. They gave my pre-op meds via the IV in my arm, and I was out.

I awakened later that day in the ICU with two chest tubes in my right chest along with the usual monitoring equipment. A large bandage covered my right chest. Surprisingly, I was very comfortable—until I took a deep breath. It felt like a Bowie knife had been impaled in my chest. Sallie was there, and Dr. Schorn arrived to brief me on the procedure's outcome. He said, "Dan, I've got some good news and some bad news." Yes, he really said that.

"Give me the bad news first," I answered.

He replied, "The tumor is malignant." *Wham!* Well, my initial fears were confirmed. He continued: "Non-small cell adenocarcinoma, stage IIB." He related that the tumor was in the periphery of the right upper lobe and had caused some puckering of the visceral pleura, or lining, of the lung, but that it had not invaded the chest wall. For that reason he abandoned the thorascopic portion of the procedure to avoid spillage of the tumor into the chest cavity. He instead resorted to the open excision of the right upper lobe to remove the entirety of the tumor without risking inadvertent spread by attempting the biopsy with the scope. This involved entering the chest through the ribs and spreading them, and using an incision from the scapula (shoulder blade) to the right nipple area, anteriorly (in the front), to expose the lung. Then the lobe of the lung was removed at its base near the posterior (back) aspect of the heart with the tumor *in situ* (in its place). Blood vessels were coagulated to stop bleeding. The bronchus, or airway tube, was ligated, or sutured, to prevent an air leakage. Chest tubes were inserted to prevent air from accumulating around the lungs, and the wound was closed.

All of this was routine information, physician to physician.

"And the good news?" I managed to ask.

Smiling, he replied, "I think we got all of it." He proceeded to describe how he had removed a number of

"AND THE GOOD NEWS?" I MANAGED TO ASK. SMILING, HE REPLIED, "I THINK WE GOT ALL OF IT."

lymph nodes from the base of the lung, the mediastinum, to be tested for possible spread of the tumor. The initial report of the frozen section, done during the surgery, was negative for spread, but the final report would follow in two to three days.

Dr. Schorn reminded me that I was "a blessed man." His point was that if we had not discovered the cancer now, within the next six months it would have enlarged and spread, making it incurable.

I was relieved—sort of. The confirmation of malignancy was bad, of course. But the news of a complete excision and no nodes positive for metastatic disease was great. I had already surrendered to the likelihood of the tumor being malignant from the pre-operative appearance on the chest X-ray and the pre-op testing results. The cell type, non-small cell adenocarcinoma, told me that complete surgical excision carries the best chance of survival since this type of tumor is less responsive to chemotherapy and not responsive at all to radiation therapy. This is quite unlike small cell carcinomas, which have a better response to radiation and, to a lesser degree, chemotherapy, but are usually more centrally located, rendering surgical excision more difficult or even impossible. (Sorry if all this sounds confusing! Just take it as free medical information.)

So after a few days in the hospital, the chest tubes

would be removed, and I could go home. Except, as seemingly happens with all physicians and medical personnel who become patients, there would be issues. The first chest tube was pulled on Post-op Day 2 without incident. I was moved to a regular room floor where I spent the next two weeks bored and hurting from the procedure.

But the second chest tube continued to leak air from my chest cavity. Each morning Dr. Schorn, or one of his colleagues, would check the tube and verify that there was still a leak present. This meant another day in the hospital. This went on day after day. Coughing and deep breathing exercises are brutal with an indwelling chest tube. But the nursing staff did its job well, not allowing me to wiggle out of anything just because I was a physician (though I reminded them often!).

During that time, I was as mobile as I could expect to be. Walking the halls, carrying my chest tube bottle like a piece of luggage, I conversed with the nurses and had numerous visitors. I think half of my church family came by. My Emmaus brothers brought Saturday morning breakfast one weekend.

One morning, Dr. Schorn asked if I wanted to go home with the chest tube in place and follow up weekly in his office until the leak stopped and the tube could be removed. Sallie and I agreed; we were anxious to return home. As a surgeon, it was easy to care for the tube and clean it daily—but sleeping at home with a chest tube is quite another experience.

Every deep breath brings pain. Each inhalation causes the tube to rub on the lining of the chest cavity, the pleura. The pleura is richly innervated by nerves and therefore extremely painful. It is a sharp pain, as described above, like a knife being forced into your chest. And heaven forbid a cough or sneeze! I slept the next several weeks in my easy chair on my left, uninvolved, side, curled up as quiet as a mouse!

And then, three weeks later, the leak disappeared. Dr. Schorn pulled my chest tube during an office visit, along with the staples in the incision, and I was released to consult an oncologist for follow-up treatment of my diagnosis.

One down! One to go!

Ten

CHEMOTHERAPY

It required six weeks to heal the incision from the surgery to remove the tumor. Usually chemotherapy and/or radiotherapy are delayed until the primary incision heals to prevent dehiscence, or a reopening of the wound. During that time Sallie and I met with several oncologists to hear various opinions as to the necessary follow-up treatment of this cancer.

After hearing similar treatment plans, but very different approaches to the process, we decided to trust my treatment to Dr. Margie Sunderland. Some of the oncologists were matter of fact, blunt, even seemingly distant of the process. Dr. Sunderland seemed to be the person placed in our path who offered the most hope and kindness during that dark period of dealing with cancer. I like to think she was one of those angelic folks we encountered during this tough time.

Most of all, she and Sallie hit it off quite well. At this moment of our lives, this was extremely important to us. Sallie reminded me of something Dr. Sunderland said that made a huge impression on her. When addressing the prognosis of the cancer and its likelihood of recurrence and morbidity, she asked, "Do you want to spend the time remaining in your life living or dying?" Her point was that, obviously, none of us knows how many days we have in this life. How we spend them is a choice all of us make daily. What a beautiful thought! It made an impression on me as a physician to grant my patients more empathy when dealing with this terrifying diagnosis we call cancer. It also taught me to never dim the flicker of hope that remains in each person, regardless of their prognosis. It is our job as physicians to embody that hope for our patients.

IT ALSO TAUGHT ME TO NEVER DIM THE FLICKER OF HOPE THAT REMAINS IN EACH PERSON, REGARDLESS OF THEIR PROGNOSIS. IT IS OUR JOB AS PHYSICIANS TO EMBODY THAT HOPE FOR OUR PATIENTS.

All of this was a vastly new experience for me. As a physician, I had dealt with patients with various stages of cancer throughout my career. As a patient, it is totally different. I learned many things during this illness, but the most important was patience. As an orthopedic surgeon, I was not satisfied with delays in treatments or scheduling. I demanded immediate attention and action for my patients. But dealing with these issues from the "other side" was a totally new experience for me. In the medical world, orthopedic surgeons are stereotyped to be notoriously impatient. On the grand scale of physicians, we probably rank last in patience when it comes to patient care. It is exhibited by the very specialty we have chosen. If a bone is broken, we fix it. If a ligament is torn, we reconstruct it. It is immediate feedback. Rarely do we have to wait for other factors before we intercede. We have been trained from residency to be action-directed. Stabilize the fracture so healing can begin. It's innately driven into every orthopedic surgeon. In short—and please pardon the pun—this impatience is in our bones.

ONE OF THEM ACTUALLY NEVER RECOGNIZED SALLIE AS BEING PRESENT IN OUR VISIT. WHAT A MISTAKE!

Our colleagues, on the other hand, must rely on patience more often than us. Oncologists are—usually—a great example of this. As I noted above, several of the oncologists we visited before treatment were not very patient or compassionate in the plan they presented. One of them actually never recognized Sallie as being present in our visit. What a mistake! As physicians, I think one of our greatest gifts to our patients is the respect, compassion, and hope we can project in their times of great stress. And that includes the *entire* family. After all, they are going through this confusing and frightening time along with the patient. To my colleagues, please let us be cognizant of the fear and confusion of the family members and friends who are so close to the patient during these times. They are the caregivers who will be with the patient each day providing for their every need. A small recognition of their presence and importance goes a long way.

Likewise, other specialties must rely on patience to do their jobs well. Internal medicine physicians must try various medications to alter physiological as well as pathological processes. Patience is a great virtue in these practices. And I know of no specialty more patient than pediatricians, dealing with crying babies and frantic parents all day long. I cannot think of a more stressful scenario. The list goes on. Cardiologists, family practice, psychiatrists, radiologists, and more—all tend to exhibit much more patience than orthopedists.

So, for me, patience was a new thing. Remember earlier I wrote about the "captain of the ship" doctrine? In surgical specialties, we, the surgeons, are expected to take charge. Diagnose the problem, formulate the treatment plan, and institute that plan to aid the healing process. I was a living example of that mentality! It would take a while to change. But change it would.

As we met with Dr. Sunderland, the treatment plan became clear. My diagnosis was confirmed as adenocarcinoma stage IIB right lung. The final report on the lymph nodes taken at the surgery was negative for tumor metastases, or spreading. But with the lack of a good margin on the surface of the lung, she and Dr. Schorn altered the staging to the next level for safety. With the excision, the only thing left was a course of chemotherapy to attempt to eradicate any leftover cells that might be hiding elsewhere in my body. Dr. Sunderland formulated a plan with several powerful chemotherapy drugs that would cause me to be nauseous, lethargic, depress my immune system, and lose my hair and the lining of my gut. Wonderful news! I could hardly wait! (Please note the obvious sarcasm I felt at the time.)

The regimen meant an all-day infusion, via IV, every three weeks for four cycles to start. With reassessment, we would decide how long to continue. I was ready, or so I thought.

* * * * *

The first infusion day was uneventful except for the presence of the other patients who were getting their infusions the same day. I saw some gaunt, blank, and ashen faces that didn't seem to show much hope as well as other faces that were smiling, courageous, almost defiant. What a difference attitude makes! Some were choosing to "live," and

WHAT A DIFFERENCE ATTITUDE MAKES! SOME WERE CHOOSING TO "LIVE," AND SOME WERE ALREADY RESIGNED TO EXIST OTHERWISE, JUST AS DR. SUNDERLAND HAD SAID.

some were already resigned to exist otherwise, just as Dr. Sunderland had said. There were all kinds of hats, scarfs, and head coverings since very few of the patients had hair. Colorful blankets with personalized lettering were scattered throughout the infusion room. Some patients were talkative while others remained silent, somnolent in their chairs.

I was determined to keep my head up and meet this head on. But I was the newbie! This being my first infusion, I didn't know what to expect. But I think the experience was more disconcerting to Sallie than me. The environment, the equipment, and the staff were all very routine for me as a physician but quite the opposite for my bride. I'm sure she was mortified at the sight of folks in various stages of their treatment who were present that day. Some would not be there the next time we came for a treatment. Others would endure treatment after treatment for months.

It is a very sobering experience.

The infusion began at 8 a.m. and lasted until 5 p.m. It is a very full day. First, there is always lab work. Blood samples are taken and tests run. Then you visit the pharmacy area to verify the drugs you will be given during that visit. Finally, the IV is started. The fluids are cold in your bloodstream, so a blanket is welcomed. We had a light lunch and talked, read, and watched TV to pass the time. There were no adverse effects that day, so we were hopeful that perhaps I would be spared some of the side effects I knew were waiting. The time passed and, by very late afternoon, we were on our way home.

No problem, I thought. That was Monday.

NO PROBLEM, I THOUGHT. THAT WAS MONDAY.

Tuesday wasn't bad, either. I thought all the symptoms I heard from patients through the years were exaggerated. I had a little queasiness, but the anti-nausea medication worked very well. So I began to wonder if all these stories were not magnified regarding their severity.

Wednesday: forget everything I just wrote. *Sick* is not descriptive enough for how I felt. If not for the meds to relieve the nausea, I would have thrown up my toenails. (That is East Texas jargon for "The nausea was so bad, if possible, I would have completely emptied my gastro-intestinal tract!") The medications would take the edge off, but the deep, burning ache in your gut is still there. Food was out of the question. Any thought of food and even the smell of food being prepared escalated the nausea. During these days, after each infusion cycle, Sallie would become my rescuer. She tried numerous dishes that used to be my favorites. I tolerated none of them well. She tirelessly kept trying.

After the fifth day, the nausea resided to a tolerable level to allow the eating of small meals. By the tenth day, I began to rebound, or so I thought. That made the second week tolerable. But entering the third week, the foreboding of the next infusion sets in. Then, the process repeats.

Each cycle gets a little worse than the previous one. I had no energy. The mind is willing for activity, but the body is not. It's as if there is no gas in the engine. There is dizziness. Your body aches all over. Starting with the second cycle, my hair fell out in clumps. During one of my showers, I suddenly found my hands full of hair! You lose your eyelashes and eyebrows. Body hair disappears. My fingernails no longer grew. Sores in my mouth had to be addressed.

Diarrhea is common since the lining of cells in the gastrointestinal tract, killed by the chemotherapy, have to be passed. You have to be careful not to dehydrate, so you drink even when you are not thirsty. Your fastest-growing cells are the first to go. That includes your hair, bone marrow, blood cells, and intestinal lining. And hopefully, any cancer cells that are growing faster than normal cells will be killed. The theory is that the cancer cells, dividing at an exponentially rapid rate, will be killed first. Unfortunately, some of your organ systems described above have rapidly dividing cells as well. These too die, causing the phenomena and side effects noted previously.

I began to experience numbness in my hands and feet from a peripheral neuropathy linked to one of the platinum-based drugs I was receiving. Peripheral neuropathy is damage to the nerves that provide sensation, temperature perception, and regulation of vascular supply to your hands and feet. These symptoms begin initially in the hands and feet, then progress to your arms and legs, and lastly inch their way toward your trunk. Some of the chemotherapy drugs have the side effect of affecting these nerves causing temporary, or sometimes permanent, damage. Thank goodness, the numbness in my hands resolved following the cessation of the chemotherapy. Otherwise, I never could have returned to my beloved work as a surgeon. I would not have been able to feel the instruments in my hands. Some numbness in my feet remains to this day as a residual finding; it continues to remind me daily of this event in my life.

Chemotherapy also affects your temperature control. I don't know the exact mechanism, although I suspect it has an effect on your central thermostat in the midbrain area or the hypothalamus. I don't tolerate extreme heat or cold like I did before the cancer. Living in Texas, summers are brutal and air-conditioning is a necessity. With chemotherapy, intolerance to heat is even more exaggerated. I used to love snow skiing, but I cannot tolerate cold temperatures anymore. Some might argue it's because I'm older, but it began immediately during the chemotherapy sessions and has not resolved to this day. So my advice to all patients who are embarking on a chemotherapy journey: keep your socks and mittens close in the winter and learn to love shade, fans, air-conditioning, and plenty of hydration in the summer.

My white blood cell count dropped tremendously, but I was aided by an injectable stimulant given after each infusion. Otherwise, interaction with other people would have been compromised due to my reduced immune response. If your white blood cell count is too low, you cannot fight infection. A simple cold can lead to a fatal event. In the event of an extremely low white blood cell count, one must isolate themselves from anyone who could transmit any communicable disease. I am so thankful I did not have to endure a mandatory isolation.

When I did shave, infrequently since my hair grew so slowly, I learned to use an electric shaver. Any nicks or cuts can lead to entrance portals for infection. My red blood cell count also plummeted, resulting in a profound anemia and reducing my ability to carry oxygen to my body. I was so tired. I passed out just getting up to go to the bathroom. I felt awful. Now I know what my patients had been describing to me all these years. Dealing with anemia is tough. What brave souls they are for tolerating these chemical onslaughts.

To actually experience this was a lesson in patience. I couldn't control what was being done or the symptoms and side effects it was producing. It was a necessary evil. In order to ensure no cancer remained, the chemotherapy needed to be done. So we continued with the process.

It certainly brought Sallie and me closer. Her relentless care for me was overwhelming. She saved me with her homemade banana pudding. It was the only thing I could tolerate during the days following the infusions. I would have to use plastic spoons since the usual silverware would leave a nasty metallic taste in my mouth, a side effect of the chemo drugs. We would have our midnight snacks of a few bites of banana pudding and talk

IT CERTAINLY BROUGHT SALLIE AND ME CLOSER. HER RELENTLESS CARE FOR ME WAS OVERWHELMING. SHE SAVED ME WITH HER HOMEMADE BANANA PUDDING.

about the "what ifs" that were looming on the horizon.

It was extremely sobering thinking about the "what ifs." What if this didn't work? What if the cancer returns? What if I'm not here? What would Sallie and the kids do? When I took down the Christmas lights that year, I specially labeled them so that if I wasn't there the next year, my son would know how to arrange them properly. I changed financial accounts to make it easier for Sallie to manage finances. I wanted to leave instructions for her to carry on if I wasn't around. The daily and monthly duties of caring for the kids, paying bills, and balancing the checkbook would have to be passed to her.

We took in as many of my middle daughter's soccer games as possible that spring. Sometimes it involved sitting in the car in the parking lot just to hear the cheers. I was unable to tolerate the cold, wet conditions outside for fear of catching a cold or flu. We were blessed to watch the Marcus girls' soccer team win the state championship in 2005, her senior year of high school! What a remarkable achievement and a happy time during an otherwise dismal period.

My son was in college, and my youngest daughter was involved in volleyball, so we tried to spend as much time as possible with their activities. We tried to not vary from our normal routines if possible. We did anything we could do to avoid disruption in their lives. Family time became more treasured than before. But worry always lingered. It always followed the thought of *What if . . . ?*

It's as if your life is placed on hold. Things that are

DANNY K. CORBITT, MD

previously important, such as work and image, no longer hold that position. Little things, often overlooked before, now become a priority. On some of the more difficult nights, I would still be awake at dawn to enjoy a sunrise I would have ignored in the past.

Finally, my kidney functions started to show signs of toxicity to the chemotherapy. My blood tests for kidney function started to rise. With a significant elevation in the BUN (blood urea nitrogen) and creatinine levels, the kidneys were starting to show damage from the side effects of the chemotherapy drugs. Thankfully, we had to cease any more infusions. Unfortunately, some of the sequelae, or permanent changes, remain as permanent reminders. The levels of function of my kidneys have stabilized but are more elevated than before chemotherapy.

* * * * *

Overall, I felt as if I had been wrapped in a cocoon. I felt isolated from the world, from the depressing effects of the chemotherapy, and from the fear the cancer had posed. I had been told, "It will be all right." And I took that at its face value. It *would* be all right, no matter the outcome. I

THERE ARE SO MANY HURDLES TO OVERCOME ALONG THE WAY THAT DEPRESSION AND ANGER ONLY SEEM TO MAKE THE JOURNEY WORSE. I WAS GIVEN A NEW PERSPECTIVE.

think a good attitude is essential for dealing with this thing we call cancer. We adopted Dr. Sunderland's advice to spend our days "living" and not "dying."

There are so many hurdles to overcome along the way that depression and anger only seem to make the journey worse. I was given a new perspective. Each day has its own merits, its own beauty, its own purpose. Sunrises and sunsets became more beautiful. It is much easier to stop and smell the roses along this journey. Each day is another day to thank God for this day that was not promised.

Eleven

ALL IN

Chemotherapy continued its seemingly endless cycles through the spring and into the early summer of 2005. I didn't have nearly the length of chemotherapy as some of my patients, however. I am grateful for that! It brought a newfound respect for these warriors who were battling a similar enemy. I was blessed to be able to stop after the fourth course of the drugs. And it was not only a fortunate thing, it was practically a necessary thing. I told Sallie on our trip to the infusion center for the fourth round that if any more was recommended I would not participate. I sometimes felt I would rather die! And I meant it!

There were times I would simply curl up in a ball and ask God if all this was really necessary. To say I found a new respect for my patients who had to continue for longer treatment courses would be an understatement. These folks were dealing with all the things I mentioned above, time and time again, for months or even years. Heaven forbid if there was a recurrence and it would have to be started all over again. I would not wish this on anyone. All of you combatants have my utmost respect.

THERE WERE TIMES I WOULD SIMPLY CURL UP IN A BALL AND ASK GOD IF ALL THIS WAS REALLY NECESSARY.

Over the next few months, I tried to regain my strength and attempt to return to work. Until the numbness resolved from my hands, though, as I said, I couldn't do surgery. I began to see patients in the office once again but had to refer them to my partners for surgery. Thankfully, the sensation in my hands did return to normal, and my days as an orthopedic surgeon resumed. I had left my practice in good hands. Beth, my assistant, my right-hand girl, had done a wonderful job managing the practice in my absence. My partners covered any problems that arose. All was right with the world! I was ready to return.

I began to reflect on several things that had occurred during this phase of my life. I tried to share my experience with anyone who would listen. I told my story to Sunday school classes, Bible studies, at various church services, and even the local Lions Club. After all, how many people have a kidney stone to get them to a hospital, where they then undergo a chest X-ray they are not supposed to have? An X-ray that shows a tumor they did not know existed? A tumor that, if not diagnosed quickly, would spread rapidly and cause death in six to twelve months? Who needs a problem for which their earthly accumulation of wealth, influence, and power provides absolutely no answers? A conflict that brings them to a point of surrender to a divine entity that loves them and is trying to answer a prayer voiced three years earlier?

Wow!

So, let's recap.

I did have a kidney stone, having never experienced one before or since. It forced me to the hospital to get a chest X-ray I was sure I didn't need. We found a tumor silently growing in my right lung that showed to be malignant and greater than 3 centimeters in diameter. That placed it in a category where metastasis was likely and the natural progression could be fatal in six to twelve months. All my means of money, position, and any ability to purchase a solution were suddenly futile.

GOD HAD GIVEN ME A PROBLEM FOR WHICH I HAD NO ANSWER.

God had given me a problem for which I had no answer.

That conflict drove me to a place I would not have come to on my own. At least, I had not come to that place during the three years since my prayer in December 2001. Through God's providence, I reached a place of surrender. I thought I was "all in" when I prayed that prayer three years earlier, but I had been wrong. In this poker game of life, I still had chips hidden in my vest pocket, just in case I needed them. What I learned was God requires total surrender to live in the close relationship I longed and prayed for. What I didn't know was the cost required to get there. When our Lord spoke to the rich young ruler in the Gospel of Luke, He told him, "Sell all that thou hast, and distribute unto the poor, and thou shalt have treasure in heaven: and come, follow me" (Luke 18:22, KJV).

Jesus didn't care about the young ruler's money. After all, He owns the entire universe! If we think the material things we accumulate in this life are ours, we are sadly mistaken. We are only temporary stewards of the riches God has provided us. We can't take them with us. We are in charge of them only for a short time. What we do with them is what is important. For that reason, Jesus did not want the young man's money. He wanted his heart.

All of it.

He's not after only the parts we are willing to share.

He wants all of it.

Including that dark little corner we want to keep for ourselves.

All of it.

In order for Him to come and abide with us, He demands total access to our lives. And being the perfect gentleman, He will not enter unless invited. He will not force His way into your heart. He's not going to kick down the door. He will stand at the door and knock (Revelation 3:20). But remember, the handle of the door is *on the inside*. You have to open it! I wasn't ready to

I WASN'T READY TO DO THAT IN DECEMBER 2001 WHEN I PRAYED FOR SOMETHING I GREATLY UNDERVALUED. I DIDN'T KNOW THE COST OF SURRENDER.

do that in December 2001 when I prayed for something I greatly undervalued. I didn't know the cost of surrender. And I certainly wasn't about to give everything up without a reason.

Well, I got my reason.

That morning before the surgery when I fought with God, I finally realized that His delay in answering my prayer was because I was not ready. Until I was placed in a position that afforded no way out, I had not been willing to completely surrender. No matter how much money I had, how many friends and colleagues I could muster, where in the world I could go, I had nothing of value to my God except my heart. My little attempt at "Let's Make a Deal" fell flat and was met with silence until I gave up. Until I relinquished the right to myself, He could not help me.

We all possess the "right to ourselves." God has given us the choice to do as we wish with the gift of grace He offers. We are allowed to be smug and prideful in retaining the right to ourselves, or we can surrender that right to allow Him to fill us with His grace. If there is a void in your heart, He will fill it. If something, such as that right to one's self, is retained there, occupying that space, He will not enter. That space may be occupied by pride, self-control, or any idea we think gives us value or bargaining power with the Almighty. When we realize we possess nothing He doesn't already own, then, and only then, can we approach Him. He will stand at the door and knock, but He won't ever force His way into your heart.

When I gave up everything, every right to my being, He hugged me and reassured me that *"It will be all right."*

That surrender allowed the hug, the sweet reply that "it will be all right," and the knowledge that He wanted that intimate relationship long before I did.

Twelve

MY UTMOST FOR
HIS HIGHEST

Let's fast-forward again. As I was recovering from the chemotherapy and had returned to work, I continued to reread my daily devotional. The cover of my copy of *My Utmost for His Highest* was becoming somewhat worn. I had been reading it since May 2001 and now it was December 2005. The surgery was over, the chemotherapy completed. I was back at work. And I had found a new relationship with God, one that I never thought possible.

On the morning I was anticipating the daily devotional I loved so much, I could not wait to reread it and finally answer "yes!" to the question of the newfound relationship with my God. As I read the final paragraph, circled in red, I was as giddy as a schoolchild with a new show-and-tell trinket.

I WAS AS GIDDY AS A SCHOOLCHILD WITH A NEW SHOW-AND-TELL TRINKET.

The idea is not that we do work for God, but that we are so loyal to Him that He can do His work through us—'I reckon on you for extreme service, with no complaining on your part and no explanation on Mine.' God wants to use us as He used His own Son.

What a comfort to see those words in print once again. I got excited. I actually began laughing at the thought that, in the past year, God had brought me to the point in which I could experience that relationship "with no complaining on your part and no explanation on Mine."

What I had asked in 2001, He answered in December and January of 2004–2005. Then my eyes scrolled to the top of the devotional page.

"December 18."

The date of my favorite devotional was December 18.

Wait. What was significant about *December 18*? Then it hit me: exactly one year earlier, on December 18, 2004, I was in the emergency room with a kidney stone and getting a chest X-ray!

That X-ray diagnosed the tumor I didn't know I had. The essential X-ray that exposed the cancer that brought me to surrender my all to my God. It was the same surrender that opened up the intimate relationship with God I had asked for in my 2001 prayer. The relationship that is the arm-in-arm, "Father, what do we do today?" closeness that exists even today was finalized with the series of events that began on December 18, 2004!

I got goose bumps.

You know, the dermatological response to excitement or temperature caused by the tiny Arrectores Pilorum muscles pulling on the hair follicles resulting in the vertical orientation of the hairs themselves! (Sorry, more doctor talk!)

I practically ran to the folder I kept with all the medical records of the events from earlier that year. And there it was. The chest X-ray report from Medical Center of Lewisville documenting the presence of a mass in the right upper lobe of my lung. Dated: *December 18, 2004!*

What a confirmation! Of all the days He picked to gift me with a kidney stone! It was a God wink. A subtle response from our heavenly Father to tell me how much He loves me and cares for my every need—as He does for every one of His children. It was a reminder that He is involved in our daily lives. Of the 365 days in the year, He chose this one day to confirm to me the loving nature and reliability of His promises. Remember the lesson on Abraham? How God took care of the small details in order to show Abraham how much He was involved in his life? Jesus told us in Luke 12:7, "Indeed, the very hairs of your head are all numbered." Yes, it had been three years. But He promises to answer our prayers that are uplifted in accordance with His will. And He did! On the very day! Three years later—in His time, and in His way, He did.

What a coincidence, you might think. Well, I don't believe in coincidences. A coincidence is when God chooses to remain anonymous. If He wants to claim credit, you can call it a miracle. I think everything happens for a reason. Some things are good, some bad.

> I DON'T BELIEVE IN COINCIDENCES. A COINCIDENCE IS WHEN GOD CHOOSES TO REMAIN ANONYMOUS.

I firmly believe He has a plan for our lives and for this world He has created. And I believe His plan will be completed regardless of whether we choose to participate or not.

You may disagree, and it is certainly your right to do so. But if you have read this far, I ask you to go just a little farther.

Thirteen

THERE ARE *NO* COINCIDENCES

I pray you have elected to read on and hear my opinion that I believe there are *no* coincidences. As I previously wrote, and believe, "A coincidence is when God chooses to remain anonymous."

As a physician and scientist, I do not believe in chance. Some would argue that there exist games of chance, that most natural forces essentially come down to this. I would counter that, for most occurrences, there are plausible explanations. Let's take a game of chance: a pair of dice is rolled. It is a function of gravity and vector forces that the thrower exerts on the dice as well as the composition of the dice that decide on which side the dice land. Can it be predicted? Nope. There are probabilities of what the landing will be. But for each individual roll, the probability begins again. One would argue that "eventually" a certain result will occur. Does it have to? Nope. Probability says it "probably" will happen, but it cannot *guarantee* that result. Nor on which roll it will occur. Each roll is independent of the one before or after.

As a scientist, I love to explain things. I love to see proof, to reproduce results in a predictable manner. I love to observe and describe things, to place them in categories or "boxes" that coincide with my understanding of how it should be. It makes me feel important and powerful if I can predict something before it happens.

I do not believe science and a belief in God are mutually exclusive. On the contrary, I believe the deeper we dive into our revelations in nature, the more we see a divine order. I think we are only scratching the surface of what remains to be revealed with today's methods of discovery. Undoubtedly, we will make tremendous advances as we probe deeper into this marvelous universe.

> I BELIEVE THE DEEPER WE DIVE INTO OUR REVELATIONS IN NATURE, THE MORE WE SEE A DIVINE ORDER.

I choose to believe in order. I think nature has a design and a purpose. My study of the human body, its anatomy and function, tends to reinforce that belief. As I stated earlier, we are "fearfully and wonderfully made" (Psalm 139:14). There are no wasted spaces in the construction of our bodies. Each organ system has a place and responsibility to each other. The systems are dependent on each other for the survival of the entire organism. Their design is genius.

Take, for instance, the simplicity of the red blood cell. What is the maximum surface area that can be obtained in the smallest volume or space to carry oxygen? The answer is a sphere. Now take a ball or sphere and deflate it. It folds on itself taking up much less total volume but retaining the same surface area for oxygen diffusion as a fully inflated sphere. That is the shape of our red blood cells. They can move into smaller spaces—that is, capillaries—while carrying the maximum amount of oxygen for cell metabolism. What an ingenious solution.

So is that mere chance? I don't think so.

The more we learn, the more we find out we don't know. It is mind-boggling to consider that DNA, which is a complete road map or blueprint to your entire body, is contained in every cell. Every cell! We have trillions of cells! Studies tell us there are more than 27 trillion at last approximation. We know through cloning that the DNA from a single cell can be reproduced to produce a new organism. What a complex and wonderful chain of molecules! To have that amount of information stored in every cell is incredible. Do I, a physician and scientist, think that happened by random chance? Hardly.

As scientists we observe, record, reproduce results through experimentation, and predict outcomes. However, we do not create *de novo* (from nothing). We alter existing compounds, atomic structures, and materials, but do we create the substrate from which they are derived? Of course not. Someone or something had to provide that substrate and the "spark," or catalyst, to make it work. Let's consider the much-debated Big Bang Theory. I don't profess to know if it happened. After all, I wasn't there. But if it did, what exploded? There had to be gaseous materials or matter to produce the explosion. Where did *they* originate? And who put them there? Did it just happen? Who pushed the button? Who provided the substrate and "the spark"?

I know, as humans, we do not like to admit there is a higher power. But I cannot, as a scientist and physician, explain innumerable phenomena. Just because you don't see something or cannot explain it, does that mean it doesn't exist? Sometimes our pride as humans gets in the way. We feel the need to explain everything in a logical, scientific way that is acceptable to us. It makes us feel better thinking we know how things work. There is an innate power in the ability to predict an event beforehand. We desire and pursue it. We laud it over others who may be less knowledgeable or educated. And we revel in that power.

But sometimes we have to admit: we just don't know.

As a physician, I see the same phenomenon with the

passing of a patient from this life. The materials of the body are still there. The brain, the heart, the lungs, the blood are all still present in death, just as they were in life, moments before. But "the spark" of life is gone. To my colleagues, yes, the defibrillator is often tried. But in the cases of death, it doesn't work. All the CPR protocols were followed, and yet the patient expired. We physicians have all been there. What changed? All the materials were present, but the body would not work. Despite all our efforts, we could not make it live. It could not be revived. Why not?

Allow me to provide another example of the incredible complexity of life. As an orthopedic surgeon, I have been privileged to witness the miracles of God daily. It is remarkable to see a young child, in follow-up for a healing forearm fracture, begin, in just two to three weeks, to show the signs of fracture callus formation. When we follow it further, it begins to remodel to its original shape. Initially there is a bump, a thickening, at the healing site. After one to two years, you cannot visibly discern the site of the original fracture.

To my colleagues, I can recite Wolff's Law. What German Julius Wolff did, in the late nineteenth century, was describe the phenomena of bone adapting its shape to forces of stress. He observed and explained it, but he didn't create it. This phenomena is a miraculous display of nature at work. I find it entertaining to ask my young patients, as I do frequently, as I show them their X-rays, if they had read a book telling them how to heal their fracture. The look of awe on their faces is priceless! As if they had experienced a miracle right before their eyes.

And, well, they had. Did I, as an orthopedist, cause this healing to happen? Of course not. I witnessed God's plan to allow the body to heal itself. Fracture healing, along with other healing, is a miraculous thing. As physicians, we try to control the environment at the healing site through surgery, bracing, casting, or wound care. Sometimes we claim success. But did we cause the body to heal? No. Personally, I think it is part of a miraculous design.

For that reason, I believe our lives are planned. I think we are a part of a master plan that controls the universe. Some of my colleagues will think I am oversimplifying this concept. In *Star Wars* terminology, they'll think I've gone to the Dark Side. Quite the contrary: I've seen the Light! The Force! I think we have a choice to adhere to and be part of this plan or refuse and allow it to happen without us. The end result will be the same. The master plan will happen with or without you. You can choose to enjoy the blessings that are offered all around us each day as part of the plan or continue to fight against it. And you can live out the frustration of working for something you can never achieve on your own. That is certainly what I was doing for so many years.

I have a deep, genuine belief that each of our lives has a purpose. Finding and living out that purpose is our ultimate goal. And I think that purpose lies at the feet of Jesus the Christ. Here are just four Scriptures I encourage you to read: Genesis 1:26, John 1:3, Colossians 1:16, and Romans 11:36.

He is the One through whom, and for whom, all things were created.

Fourteen

Sweet Savior

In May 2007, some two years after this episode of my life, things were going great. I had been given clear checkups from my oncologist, Dr. Sunderland. We were doing our diligence to follow up on the lung cancer with regular checkups. The statistics for survival and recurrence of non-small cell adenocarcinoma are based on a four-year period.

The dread of recurrence, however, was a daily concern for me. With my surgery and chemotherapy, we had done our best to eradicate the tumor, but the regular reminders with the office visits and repeat CT scans were enough to keep the thought in the forefront of my daily routine: the cancer could reappear at any time. So I would have nightmarish bouts of fitful sleep, too often dreaming that I had to undergo that dreadful chemotherapy again. I would worry that I would not be around to care for my family. After all, I'm human, and humans worry.

I had returned to full-time work in my orthopedic practice. My family was doing great. Church activities were frequent and enjoyable. But the worry of "what if" the cancer came back remained. Then, one night, I had a dream.

I was at the foot of two great gates. They were old and wooden, made with massive beams with a very rough texture. There were no handles or latches, so there was no apparent way to open the gates. As I looked up, they were so tall they disappeared into the mist. The ancient stone walls on either side of the gates extended as far as I could see, also disappearing into the mist. The ground was barren. There was no vegetation. I was alone. And it was cold. It was a bone-chilling, shivering cold where you never seem to get warm. Leaning over, I peered into the crack between the two gates and saw a warm, bright light emanating from the other side. It was nearly blinding. Then I awoke.

> I WAS AT THE FOOT OF TWO GREAT GATES. THEY WERE OLD AND WOODEN, MADE WITH MASSIVE BEAMS WITH A VERY ROUGH TEXTURE.

Immediately, the words "Sweet Savior, lift me up to you" came into my consciousness. I jumped out of bed and began writing down song lyrics as they were dictated to me. I wrote as fast as I could. Twelve minutes later, a song was completed. The result was the answer concerning the worry I had been experiencing these past few months. I think God comforted me with the lyrics of this song; it was His way of telling me to stop worrying.

Those gates of death were not for me at this time, which is why they were closed and I had no way to open them. The bright light on the other side is my Jesus. I will revisit those gates sometime in the future and, at that point, they will open, revealing my Savior ready to meet me and take me home. As for now and all the days I have remaining on this earth, there is no need to fear. In 1 John 4:18, the Bible states, "There is no fear in love. But perfect love drives out fear."

Like you, I've not been given the exact date of that meeting. But, as He cradled my face in His hands early on the morning of my epiphany, didn't He promise, *"It will be all right"*?

Here are the lyrics He sent me:

SWEET SAVIOR

Sweet Savior, lift me up to You,
Beyond the stars above.
Let my soul soar to You,
On outstretched Wings of Love.

Sweet Savior lift me up to You,
Freed from the bonds of earth.
My wandering heart longs for You,
As a child for its Father since birth.

Chorus:
Shadows of death, around me rise
I sense not terror nor fear
Sweet Savior, lift me up to You,
And fly me away from here.

Sweet Savior, lift me up to You,
My time so short it grows.
The days I have, may I glorify You,
In Your will, not mine, shall life close.

Sweet Savior, lift me up to You,
Death's doors seem dark as night.
Keep whispering to me as you cradle my face,
"I'm the light, child . . . It will be all right."

Why, you may ask, would God send a song to an orthopedic surgeon? Good question! Although I had played guitar since high school, I had only recently become a member of a gospel bluegrass band. We formed the band about twelve years ago, after my battle with cancer, to play the old songs that were being lost in today's music world. The band was started to fill a void we had in our church for the infrequent times we wanted to do an old hymn with a bluegrass "feel."

> WHY, YOU MAY ASK, WOULD GOD SEND A SONG TO AN ORTHOPEDIC SURGEON? GOOD QUESTION!

On a dare, my good friend and I picked up the mandolin and banjo, respectively. With the addition of a wonderful vocalist and her flat-top, guitar-picking husband, we became a group. We have since added a bass player to complete the ensemble. We play at churches, gatherings, festivals, and virtually anywhere someone wants to listen. Our music is our mission. We attempt to faithfully present the Gospel through the bluegrass genre. "Sweet Savior" was recorded on our first CD. If you care to hear the lyrics along with the melody, you can contact us online at Facebook. Simply find "Cross Timbers Gospel Bluegrass Band."

There is just a bit more left to my story.

Fifteen

AREN'T WE ALL LIKE HEZEKIAH?

I invite you to read all, or one, of these passages in the
Bible. It won't take long.

- 2 Kings 18–20
- Isaiah 36–39
- 2 Chronicles 29–32

I won't bore you with the extended story of Hezekiah.
Suffice it to say he was king of Judah about 700 BC. You
can read the account in the Scripture references above.
It was during the time of the split of Israel into the
northern kingdom of Israel and the southern kingdom
of Judah. Hezekiah was a good king; he tried to rally
the people to return to God and the temple and away

from the rampant idolatry that prevailed at that time. The northern kingdom had been attacked and overrun by King Sennacherib of Assyria.

During this time, Hezekiah became ill from what is described as an infection or abscess of some kind. He was dying. He contritely prayed to God to spare his life—and God granted him another fifteen years. Sometimes I feel like Hezekiah. God has spared me and given me extra time after the cancer. At the writing of this book, it has been thirteen and one-half years since the diagnosis.

It poses the question of why I have taken so long to write this book. Why now? There are several reasons. Many folks, after hearing my story, have said I should write a book concerning these events. I had a vision or thought two years after the event in which I saw the cover and title of this compilation as vividly as I saw the sunrise this morning. But it took the unsolicited prodding of a very good friend to finally set this thing in motion.

> SOMETIMES I FEEL LIKE HEZEKIAH. GOD HAS SPARED ME AND GIVEN ME EXTRA TIME AFTER THE CANCER.

On a beach in Galveston during the fall of 2017, my friend Sonny asked his question without a hint of provocation. "When are you going to write your book?" Sonny asked.

"What book?" I replied.

"The book about the story of your cancer," Sonny calmly said.

Shocked at his insistence and the fact we had never discussed writing a book about this story, I responded just as simply. "I'll get around to it sometime," I said.

He wouldn't let me off the hook. "I'll give you one year. Then I'm going to ask you again. You need to write the book."

How he knew, why he knew, and the timing of the request are all still puzzles to me—unless you consider that maybe it's God's time to get this story in print. I had no valid argument against what Sonny was asking, so here it is. I'll leave it for you to decide.

In the time immediately after the cancer scare, I was afraid to write things down. After all, I was an orthopedic surgeon. People might think I was crazy. They might wonder if the chemotherapy had affected my ability to think rationally! I still had a medical practice to maintain. Plus, I am not a writer (as you have no doubt learned by now).

But time has softened those barriers. It has given me a new perspective. And, like Hezekiah, God has given me more time.

* * * * *

At times, I wonder why I was left here. He could have taken me at any time during the process. Without the kidney stone and X-ray, there is no doubt I would have succumbed to the natural course of malignant lung cancer in a few months. My life could have ended during surgery or in the post-op period. In the chemotherapy that followed, when I felt so weakened, I honestly had moments of wondering why I wasn't taken. (Look at the lyrics of "Sweet Savior" carefully in the previous chapter.) Certainly, I was ready to go at any time. But as I recovered, it became more obvious there was something I was supposed to do. Then he gave me the dream and the song, "Sweet Savior."

I knew He left me for a reason. I am here today to tell this story to you—*His* story.

It is, after all, God's story.

I was just the less-than-innocent bystander, the first-hand witness to His handiwork that I have shared with you. I should not be here, and wouldn't be, were it not for the amazing set of events that occurred in late 2004 and early 2005. They were events over which I had no control. By medical standards and the natural history of non-small cell adenocarcinoma of the lung, I would not have discovered the tumor in my chest until it would have been too late to remove it completely. Because it had produced no symptoms, by the time they became apparent it would have been too late. As Dr. Schorn reminded me, if the cancer had not been found within another six months, the primary tumor and its metastases would have been fatal for me sometime in 2005 or 2006 if it had followed its usual devastating course.

Because of this, I thank God for each day, each sunrise, and each sunset. Most importantly, I thank Him for being left here to communicate this story to you. For without the kidney stone, the chest X-ray I didn't want, the Abraham lesson, my epiphany, the surgery, the chemotherapy experience, and the confirmation of His "coincidental" timing with the devotional from *My Utmost for His Highest,* I would not have been given the opportunity to share this remarkable story with you.

May I present one word about my epiphany before I close? I think we each have our epiphany moments with God. Some are dramatic, like the one experienced by the apostle Paul on the Damascus Road (Acts 9). Some are subtle, delivered in the quietness or solitude of our day-to-day existence. Some people who have heard this story are concerned that they have not experienced a mountaintop encounter. That they have not had a head-spinning, knock-your-socks-off event that is complete with blinding lights, fireworks, or angelic voices. And because of this, they may feel their moment is not as valuable or as real as that of someone else.

SOME PEOPLE WHO HAVE HEARD THIS STORY ARE CONCERNED THAT THEY HAVE NOT EXPERIENCED A MOUNTAINTOP ENCOUNTER.

I would respectfully submit that the form or degree of the presentation in which God chooses to reveal Himself to you doesn't matter. We are all on our own spiritual journey and experience God in different, intimate, and unique ways. This does not make any experience more or less important than those of others. Sometimes we are more receptive to God's nudging than we might be at other points in our lives. I was obstinate, proud, and self-centered. It took a cancer diagnosis to bring me to my knees! But what a blessing to know that God cares enough to encounter us in the way we are most receptive. God speaks to us individually, in the ways we each need to hear or see or feel. Remember, Elijah didn't see God in the wind, the earthquake, or the fire that followed, but he heard Him in a quiet, gentle whisper (1 Kings 19:12). The encounter is between you and God. It is your journey. I have only shared mine.

> THE ENCOUNTER IS BETWEEN YOU AND GOD. IT IS YOUR JOURNEY.

So, we are all like Hezekiah. We have all been given extra days that have not been promised. Whether we choose to realize it, these days are gifts of God. We can use them for great things and appreciate them. Or, we can squander them seeking material things that will not last. Engaged in the whirlwind we call living, we can be too busy to see the presence of God in the small things. We never know how many days we have left. I only ask that you please use them wisely as Hezekiah did thousands of years ago.

Thank you for your perseverance in reading this far. I hope something you have read has touched you in some small way. It has been a blessing for me to get this story on paper. I hope God uses it for His glory. Certainly it is His story to use as He wants. So please do not hesitate to voice your prayers and concerns to the One who listens. Petition the Creator, who cares enough to intercede in our lives even when we don't know what we need or when we think it is needed.

I pray His blessings on you with my favorite prayer that has evolved from this time in my life:

Father, grant us the faith to recklessly
abandon ourselves to You.
To abide in Your perfect love.
And most of all, to adore You above all else.
Amen.

And remember: be careful of what you ask.
He's listening.
Then hang on for the answer!

Notes

1. Oswald Chambers, *My Utmost for His Highest* (New York, New York: Dodd, Mead, and Company, Inc., 1935), p. 353.

2. Squire Rushnell, *When God Winks at You: How God Speaks Directly to You Through the Power of Coincidence* (Nashville: Thomas Nelson, 2006).

3. Rev. Tommy Nelson's devotional, presented at Lakeland Baptist Church, January 11, 2005.